M

by Iain Gray

LangSyne
PUBLISHING
WRITING *to* REMEMBER

LangSyne
PUBLISHING
WRITING *to* REMEMBER

79 Main Street, Newtongrange,
Midlothian EH22 4NA
Tel: 0131 344 0414 Fax: 0845 075 6085
E-mail: info@lang-syne.co.uk
www.langsyneshop.co.uk

Design by Dorothy Meikle
Printed by Printwell Ltd

ISBN 978-1-85217-425-5

Murdoch

MOTTO:
Under favourable auspices
(and) All things for the good.

CREST:
The head of a lion
(and) The head of a savage
impaled on a sword.

NAME variations include:
Murdock
MacMurdoch
MacMurdack
Murdoson

Chapter one:

The origins of the clan system

by Rennie McOwan

The original Scottish clans of the Highlands and the great families of the Lowlands and Borders were gatherings of families, relatives, allies and neighbours for mutual protection against rivals or invaders.

Scotland experienced invasion from the Vikings, the Romans and English armies from the south. The Norman invasion of what is now England also had an influence on land-holding in Scotland. Some of these invaders stayed on and in time became 'Scottish'.

The word clan derives from the Gaelic language term 'clann', meaning children, and it was first used many centuries ago as communities were formed around tribal lands in glens and mountain fastnesses.

The format of clans changed over the centuries, but at its best the chief and his family held the land on behalf of all, like trustees, and the ordinary clansmen and women believed they had a blood relationship with the founder of their clan.

There were two way duties and obligations. An inadequate chief could be deposed and replaced by someone of greater ability.

Clan people had an immense pride in race. Their relationship with the chief was like adult children to a father and they had a real dignity.

The concept of clanship is very old and a more feudal notion of authority gradually crept in.

Pictland, for instance, was divided into seven principalities ruled by feudal leaders who were the strongest and most charismatic leaders of their particular groups.

By the sixth century the 'British' kingdoms of Strathclyde, Lothian and Celtic Dalriada (Argyll) had emerged and Scotland, as one nation, began to take shape in the time of King Kenneth MacAlpin.

Some chiefs claimed descent from ancient kings which may not have been accurate in every case.

By the twelfth and thirteenth centuries the clans and families were more strongly brought under the central control of Scottish monarchs.

Lands were awarded and administered more and more under royal favour, yet the power of the area clan chiefs was still very great.

The long wars to ensure Scotland's

independence against the expansionist ideas of English monarchs extended the influence of some clans and reduced the lands of others.

Those who supported Scotland's greatest king, Robert the Bruce, were awarded the territories of the families who had opposed his claim to the Scottish throne.

In the Scottish Borders country – the notorious Debatable Lands – the great families built up a ferocious reputation for providing warlike men accustomed to raiding into England and occasionally fighting one another.

Chiefs had the power to dispense justice and to confiscate lands and clan warfare produced a society where martial virtues – courage, hardiness, tenacity – were greatly admired.

Gradually the relationship between the clans and the Crown became strained as Scottish monarchs became more orientated to life in the Lowlands and, on occasion, towards England.

The Highland clans spoke a different language, Gaelic, whereas the language of Lowland Scotland and the court was Scots and in more modern times, English.

Highlanders dressed differently, had different

customs, and their wild mountain land sometimes seemed almost foreign to people living in the Lowlands.

It must be emphasised that Gaelic culture was very rich and story-telling, poetry, piping, the clarsach (harp) and other music all flourished and were greatly respected.

Highland culture was different from other parts of Scotland but it was not inferior or less sophisticated.

Central Government, whether in London or Edinburgh, sometimes saw the Gaelic clans as a challenge to their authority and some sent expeditions into the Highlands and west to crush the power of the Lords of the Isles.

Nevertheless, when the eighteenth century Jacobite Risings came along the cause of the Stuarts was mainly supported by Highland clans.

The word Jacobite comes from the Latin for James – Jacobus. The Jacobites wanted to restore the exiled Stuarts to the throne of Britain.

The monarchies of Scotland and England became one in 1603 when King James VI of Scotland (1st of England) gained the English throne after Queen Elizabeth died.

The Union of Parliaments of Scotland and England, the Treaty of Union, took place in 1707.

Some Highland clans, of course, and Lowland families opposed the Jacobites and supported the incoming Hanoverians.

After the Jacobite cause finally went down at Culloden in 1746 a kind of ethnic cleansing took place. The power of the chiefs was curtailed. Tartan and the pipes were banned in law.

Many emigrated, some because they wanted to, some because they were evicted by force. In addition, many Highlanders left for the cities of the south to seek work.

Many of the clan lands became home to sheep and deer shooting estates.

But the warlike traditions of the clans and the great Lowland and Border families lived on, with their descendants fighting bravely for freedom in two world wars.

Remember the men from whence you came, says the Gaelic proverb, and to that could be added the role of many heroic women.

The spirit of the clan, of having roots, whether Highland or Lowland, means much to thousands of people.

Chapter two:

Fields of battle

A name with ancient Celtic roots, 'Murdoch' is ranked at 97 in the list of the 100 most popular surnames in Scotland.

Not exclusive to any particular region, it was to be found from earliest times from Galloway in the south-west to the Western Isles and in Badenoch, Strathspey.

Also a popular forename in the form of 'Murdo', it is thought to derive from the Gaelic *muireach*, indicating 'mariner' or *murchadh*, meaning 'sea warrior'.

In Ireland, 'Murdoch' and 'Murdock' are anglicised forms of the native Irish *Gaelic Ó Muircheartaigh* – although Protestant settlers also brought the names to the island from Scotland in the seventeenth century.

Although heirs to their own proud traditions, the Murdochs of today are also recognised as a sept, or sub-branch, of two renowned Scottish clans – those of Clan Macpherson and Clan MacDonald – more properly known as Clan Donald – and, as such, entitled to wear their tartans.

As a sept of Clan Donald – one of Scotland's

largest clans and whose several branches include the MacDonalds of Sleat, Clanranald, Glengarry and Keppoch – the Murdochs shared in both their fortunes and misfortunes.

With their motto of 'By sea, by land', and crest of an armoured hand holding a cross, the MacDonalds were masters of a sprawling fiefdom, ruling a confederacy of clans while, from their base at Dunyveg on the south of Islay, they controlled a strategic sea route between the north of Ireland and Scotland's western seaboard.

Of Norse-Gaelic roots, the clan takes its name from Donald, 1st Lord of the Isles, and a grandson of the twelfth century Somerled.

By the mid-twelfth century, Somerled, or Somhairle, whose name means 'summer wanderer' or 'summer sailor', had carved out a vast west coast fiefdom that included the south isles from Bute to Ardnamurchan Point in addition to Kintyre, Argyll and Lorne.

Known as the King of the Isles and fiercely independent, he considered he owed allegiance to no man, not least the King of Scots.

It was following the death of David I in 1153 that his grandson, Malcolm, succeeded to the throne as Malcolm IV.

He inherited a troubled kingdom torn apart by not only internecine warfare on the mainland but the threat of invasion from the north by Vikings, who sacked Aberdeen in the same year that he succeeded to the throne, and invasion from the west in the form of Somerled.

A powerful group of ambitious magnates, mainly centred in the Moray area in the northeast of Scotland, resolved to depose Malcolm, replacing him with their own puppet king, and were joined in this bold venture by Somerled.

In 1157, one year after he defeated his wife's brother, Godfred, the King of Man, in a sea battle off Islay, in the Inner Hebrides, Somerled seized control of the islands of Bute and Arran.

Control of these strategically important islands increased the threat he posed to the west coast mainland and Malcolm, rather naively, sought to resolve the problem by ordering Somerled to surrender his domains into the hands of the Crown, thereafter holding them as a mere vassal.

Somerled's answer was predictable.

He assembled a 15,000 strong force of kinsmen and, embarking in a fleet of 164 swift galleys, sailed up the Firth of Clyde and then up the Clyde to sack the town of Glasgow in a blood-crazed orgy of arson, rape and plunder.

Malcolm's loyal magnate in the west, Walter Fitzalan, the High Steward, hastily assembled a rag-tag force of other loyal magnates and their retainers.

Somerled, eager to face the challenge, met the woefully inadequate royal army at Renfrew.

Accounts differ on what now actually transpired on that bitterly cold day of January 1st, 1164.

One account is that a fierce battle ensued and, as Somerled's battle-hardened Islesmen rapidly gained the upper hand over the royal forces, the tide of battle turned when Somerled received a mortal thrust from a spear.

Dismayed at the loss of their leader, the Islesmen's discipline broke down, and hundreds were slaughtered as they fled back to their galleys.

A rather less heroic account of the victory, however, is that the High Steward had realised he had no realistic hope of defeating Somerled in a set-piece battle and, accordingly, bribed Maurice MacNeill, Somerled's nephew, to murder his uncle.

MacNeill accomplished this treacherous deed by gaining admittance to Somerled's tent after his army had encamped at Renfrew and stabbed him through the heart, possibly while he slept.

Donald, grandson of Somerled, died in about 1250, and his descendants were stalwart in their support of Scotland's great warrior king Robert the Bruce, with Angus Og MacDonald and his kinsfolk fighting at his side at the battle of Bannockburn.

This was in June of 1314, when a 20,000-strong English army under Edward II was defeated by a Scots army less than half this strength.

It was as reward for Clan Donald's loyal support that Bruce rewarded them by proclaiming that, in future battles, they would be given the honoured position of fighting on the right wing of the Scots army.

Nearly 200 years later, in September of 1513, Clan Donald and their kinsfolk such as the Murdochs were on the bloody field of battle known as Flodden.

This was a truly national disaster, with an estimated 10,000 Scots who included James IV, an archbishop, two bishops, eleven earls, fifteen barons and 300 knights killed.

The clan also proved loyal to the cause of the Royal House of Stuart, supporting it throughout the abortive Jacobite Risings of 1715 and 1745.

Bearers of the Murdoch name also fought for the Stuart cause through their kinship with Clan Macpherson.

With their main territory in Badenoch, in Strathspey, and with their motto of 'Touch not the cat without a glove' and crest of a rampant wildcat, this ancient clan were also leading members of the powerful confederation of clans known as Clan Chattan.

It was Ewen Macpherson, Chief of the Macphersons, who led his clansmen and kinsmen such as the Murdochs at Culloden. Following the defeat, and with a price on his head, he spent nine long years hiding out in the rugged grandeur of Badenoch before being able to escape to France.

In addition to their close affiliation to Clan Donald of the Western Isles and Clan Macpherson of Badenoch, bearers of the Murdoch name also have a strong association with Galloway – to the extent that it explains a rather odd central motif that appears on some Murdoch Coats of Arms.

This is a motif of two ravens pierced, or transfixed, through the heads by an arrow.

The origins of this go back to the early months of 1307 when Robert the Bruce, who had been enthroned as King of Scots only about a year earlier, found himself a hunted man, closely pursued through Galloway by his enemies.

It was a time when the fortunes of the great

warrior king were at one of their lowest ebbs, and it was only because of the selfless support he received from others that he was able to rally his fortunes and, seven years later, achieve his great victory at Bannockburn.

Those who rallied to his cause, even when it appeared hopeless, included a widow woman and her three sons from Craigencallie, near Loch Dee.

The widow sheltered the fugitive king in her cottage, offering him some humble but nevertheless welcome fare, before introducing him to her sons.

Eager to impress their king, one of the lads demonstrated his astonishing archery skills by, firing only one arrow, shooting two ravens perched on a rock, both through the head. Impressed by his skill with the bow, Bruce invited him and his two brothers to join his then meagre forces.

The lads are reputed to have subsequently served him through thick and thin, ultimately being rewarded with the lands of Hassock and Cumloden, northwest of Newton Stewart, in Galloway.

It was here, known as the Murdochs of Cumloden, that the family held lands up until about the middle of the eighteenth century – with a Coat of Arms featuring two ravens transfixed through the heads by an arrow.

Chapter three:

Poetry and the press

Far from the fields of battle and recognised as having played a profound role in the educational development of Scotland's national bard Robert Burns, John Murdoch was born in Ayrshire in 1747. His influence on Burns cannot be overestimated.

It was in May of 1765 that Murdoch, then a 19-year-old student of languages, was approached by Burns' father, William, to provide educational instruction for his sons Robert and Gilbert and also for other children from the small Ayrshire village of Alloway.

With his salary paid by the parents of his young charges and their families taking it in turn to lodge and feed him, Murdoch eagerly embarked on an educational regime that taught the basics of education before introducing the study of literary English and the Old and the New Testament.

Burns, aged six when he first came under Murdoch's tutelage, thrived under the young schoolteacher's guidance, and his poetic imagination was fired when he introduced him to Arthur Masson's *A Collection of Prose and Verse, from the Best English Authors*.

The future national bard's full-time schooling under Murdoch ended after only two and a half years, when the teacher was appointed to a post at a school in Ayr.

But Murdoch still found time to visit the Burns household and devote time to the budding poet, frequently gifting him inspirational works of literature.

Never afraid to speak his mind, Murdoch lost his teaching position in Ayr after expressing controversial views over a locally prominent and influential minister of the Church of Scotland.

Leaving his native Scotland, he settled in London, eking out a meagre living as a language teacher and seller of stationery.

He and Burns maintained a regular correspondence up until the poet's early death in Dumfries in July of 1796. Murdoch survived him by 28 years, dying in extreme poverty in London in 1824.

Bearers of the Murdoch name have also imprinted their mark on the historical record through endeavours far from the land of their birth.

Born in 1850 in Paisley, George Murdoch was aged five when he left Scotland with his family to settle in Saint John, New Brunswick.

Moving to Calgary at the age of 23 and

starting a successful horse harness business, he is recognised today as having been the city of Calgary's first permanent businessman.

The main clientele for his harness equipment were the North West Mounted Police and the Blackfoot Indians, whose language he was able to master.

Serving from 1884 to 1886 as Calgary's first mayor, he died in 1910.

One of a Scots-Australian dynasty of bearers of the Murdoch name who include the media tycoon Rupert Murdoch, Professor Walter Murdoch was born in 1874.

The youngest of fourteen children of the Church of Scotland minister the Rev James Murdoch and his wife Helen, he was aged 10 when the family emigrated from Scotland to settle in Melbourne, Australia.

Becoming a leading academic and man of letters and renowned not only for his intelligence but also for his humanity, he was a chancellor and founding professor of English at the University of Western Australia, Perth, while Murdoch University, also in Perth, is named in his honour.

Also honoured with a knighthood, he died in 1970, and one of his nephews was the Australian journalist and media mogul Sir Keith Murdoch, who syndicated many of his uncle's essays through his newspaper network.

Born in Melbourne in 1885, his parents, the Rev Patrick Murdoch and his wife Annie, had emigrated from Scotland to Australia three years earlier.

Foregoing the opportunity of a university education in favour of a career in the press, the Melbourne newspaper *The Age* employed him as district correspondent for the Malvern area.

But his early career as a pressman was hampered by a stammer and shyness brought about by this impediment.

He moved to London in 1908 to undergo speech therapy, eventually and through the influence of family friends who included no less a figure than the then Australian Prime Minister Alfred Deakin, gaining employment with the London-based *Pall Mall* magazine.

Although a talented journalist, his stammer and shyness continued to prove impediments to his work and the magazine, reluctantly, dismissed him.

Undaunted, he returned to Australia and *The Age*, working for a time as its Parliamentary reporter and forging valuable relationships with figures who included the future Australian Prime Minister Andrew Fisher.

He was despatched during the First World War as a correspondent to Gallipoli, in Turkey, where Australian and New Zealand troops were among those engaged in what proved to be the senseless carnage of the Dardanelles Campaign.

He used his political connections to circumvent strict censorship and furnish the Australian government and the British Cabinet with a damning report on the conduct of the campaign.

The chilling report was also later published in British newspapers and led to Sir Ian Hamilton, commander of the Dardanelles Campaign, being relieved of command.

By 1921, Murdoch had become chief editor of the *Melbourne Herald* and he later acquired the *Sydney Sun* – destined to become Australia's biggest-selling newspaper.

Other media acquisitions followed, including radio stations, and in 1935 he formed Australian Associated Press Ltd.

Knighted in 1933, he died in 1952 and, while much of his estate had to be sold off to pay death duties, the Murdoch family was still left in full control of News Limited, proprietors of the *Adelaide News*.

His widow is Dame Elizabeth Murdoch, whom he married in 1928.

A noted philanthropist, she was born in Melbourne in 1909, her paternal grandfather having been William Greene, a Scottish railway engineer who had immigrated to Australia.

Appointed a Dame Commander of the British Empire in 1963, she is also the recipient of an honorary doctorate of laws from the University of Melbourne in recognition of her contribution to research, the arts and philanthropy.

She and her late husband had four children, one of whom is Keith Rupert Murdoch, better known as the international media tycoon Rupert Murdoch.

Born in Melbourne in 1931, and beginning with control of the *Adelaide News* following his father's death, he has risen to become chairman and chief executive of News Corporation – a global media empire that includes ownership of newspapers, radio stations and cable television networks.

Ranked in 2010 by the prestigious *Forbes* magazine as the 13th most powerful person in the world and also listed as the 117th wealthiest person in the world, he has also, sometimes controversially, enjoyed personal audiences with politicians who include former British Prime Minister Margaret Thatcher and American President Barack Obama.

Buying what was then the British broadsheet newspaper the *Sun* in 1969 and transforming it into a hugely successful tabloid, he created BskyB in 1990 by merging his satellite network Sky Television with British Satellite Broadcasting.

In 2006 his media empire itself became the centre of a storm of controversy over allegations that some of its titles, particularly the *News of the World*, the top-selling Sunday 'sister' title of the *Sun*, hacked mobile telephones to obtain titbits of information on celebrities, royalty and public citizens.

This culminated five years later, in July of 2011, when it was revealed that a private investigator had been hired by the *News of the World* to intercept the voice mail of the missing British teenager Milly Dowler, who was later found murdered.

With widespread public disgust over the revelations, News International announced the closure of the newspaper, while Murdoch resigned as its director.

It was as a condition of rules that disbar non-American citizens from owning U.S. television stations that he took up American citizenship, allowing him to set up the Fox Broadcasting Company – but as a consequence losing his Australian citizenship.

Married four times, it was through his marriage from 1967 to 1999 to his second wife, the Scots-born journalist Anna Torv, that he is the father of Elisabeth, James and Lachlan Murdoch.

Born in 1968 in Sydney, his daughter Elisabeth is the business executive who set up the British-based Shine Limited television production company in 2001.

His son James, born in 1972, holds posts that include chairman and chief executive of News Corporation for Europe and Asia, while Lachlan Murdoch, born in 1971, is a former News Corporation executive.

Chapter four:

On the world stage

There is a memorial in the small Scottish village of Dalbeattie, in Dumfries and Galloway, to one of its native sons whose name remains forever linked to tragic events that occurred thousands of miles away on April 15th, 1912, when more than 1,500 people lost their lives in one of the world's greatest maritime disasters.

Born in the village in 1873, Lieutenant William McMaster Murdoch, better known to posterity as **Will Murdoch**, is memorialised because he was the heroic First Officer aboard the White Star Line passenger vessel *Titanic* when it collided with an iceberg in the Atlantic Ocean.

From a long line of seafarers, with his father, grandfather and four great-uncles having plied the world's oceans as sea captains, he was aged only 14 when he first went to sea.

Extremely hard working and diligent, he rose rapidly through the ranks of the White Star Line and was selected as First Officer of *Titanic* for its maiden voyage to New York.

The luxury liner had set sail in a blaze of publicity, but disaster struck in the lonely wastes of the Atlantic when she struck an iceberg.

As officer in charge of the bridge at the time of the collision, Murdoch became responsible for the evacuation of passengers and crew from the starboard side of the vessel, helping to launch ten lifeboats that are reckoned to have carried about 70% of those who survived.

He was last seen attempting to launch a collapsible lifeboat just before the bridge was swamped by the merciless ocean waves.

But, despite subsequent well-documented testimony from survivors that Murdoch had heroically carried out his duties to the end, putting the lives of the passengers and his fellow crew before his own, insidious rumours later suggested that he may have had shot at panicking passengers before committing suicide by firing a revolver into his head.

Despite there being no substance to the allegations, they became the basis of a controversial scene in the 2003 James Cameron documentary film *Ghosts of the Abyss*.

The filmmakers refused to delete the scene involving Murdoch, despite vociferous complaints from his surviving relatives and his home village of Dalbeattie.

Film studio executives, however, later visited the village to issue an apology and also to donate a charitable prize that has been established in Murdoch's name – while he is also honoured by the village's own memorial to his heroism.

From the tragedy of the *Titanic* close on 100 years ago to the much different world of contemporary music, **Shirley Murdock**, born in 1957 in Toledo, Ohio, is the best-selling rhythm and blues singer whose hit singles include the 1986 *As We Lay* and the 1992 *Let There Be Love!*

The singer has also appeared in films that include the 2005 *Sweating in the Spirit* and, from 2007, *First Cousins*.

Born in London to a Scottish-French mother and a Greek father, **Alexi Murdoch** is the singer and songwriter who, after settling in the United States in 1998, has released acclaimed albums that include his 2006 *Time Without Consequence* – tracks of which have been featured in television shows that include *Dirty Sexy Money*, *The O.C.* and *Ugly Betty* and films that include the 2009 *Towards the Sun*.

Back to the original Murdoch homeland of

Scotland, **Stuart Murdoch**, born in 1968 in Clarkston, East Renfrewshire is the singer and songwriter of the band Belle and Sebastian.

Formed in 1995, their hit albums include *Dear Catastrophe* and *The Life Pursuit*.

Back across the Atlantic, and on the stage, **George Murdock** is the veteran American actor best known for playing the role of a judge.

It was in such a role, as Judge Julius Hoffman in the acclaimed stage play *The Chicago Conspiracy Trial*, that the actor, born in 1930 in Salina, Kansas, is most noted. His many television roles include *The Twilight Zone*, *The Untouchables*, *The Streets of San Francisco*, *Ironside*, *ER* and *Chicago Hope*.

A British comedy actor of radio, television and film, **Richard Murdoch** was born in 1907 in Keston, Kent.

Best known as part of a double-act with the comedian Arthur Askey on the 1938 to 1940 BBC radio programme *Band Waggon*, he later appeared in a film of the same name.

Also known for BBC radio programmes that included the 1944-1954 *Much Binding in the Marsh* and, from 1962 to 1977, *The Men from the Ministry*, he died in 1990.

Bearers of the name have also excelled in the highly competitive world of sport.

In the sport of curling, **David Murdoch** is part of a Scottish dynasty of top curlers.

Born in Dumfries in 1978 and resident in nearby Lockerbie, along with his team of Peter Smith, Euan Byers, Warwick Smith and Ewan MacDonald, he won both the 2006 and 2009 World Curling Championships.

He is the brother of the curling coach **Nancy Murdoch**, born in 1969, and of **Neil Murdoch**, born in 1972 and winner, along with himself, of the 2003 European Championships.

From the curling rink to the cricket pitch, **Billy Murdoch** was the Australian cricketer who captained his national team on tours to England in 1880 and 1882.

Regarded as one of the greatest batmen of his time, Murdoch, who was born in 1854, settled in England in 1890.

Captaining Sussex for a time and playing Test cricket for his adopted nation, he was one of only very few cricketers to have played Tests for more than one country; he died in 1911.

On the fields of European football, **Colin**

Murdock, born in 1975 in Ballymena, Co. Antrim, is the former Northern Ireland player who, in addition to playing for teams that include Manchester United and, from 2003 to 2005, Scottish club Hibernian, also earned 34 caps playing for his country between 2000 and 2006.

In the creative world of the written word, Iris Murdoch, better known as **Dame Iris Murdoch** after she was made a Dame Commander of the British Empire in 1987 for her services to literature, was the philosopher and prolific author born in Dublin in 1919.

Taking up the pen after studying classics, philosophy and ancient history at both Cambridge and Oxford universities, she went on to publish 26 novels and works of philosophy and drama.

Her first novel, the 1954 *Under the Net*, was selected two years after her death in 1999 by the editorial board of Modern Library as one of the 100 best English language novels of the twentieth century, while her many other awards include a 1973 James Tait Black Memorial Prize for her *The Black Prince* and, a year later, the Whitbread Literary Award for Fiction for *The Sacred and Profane Love Machine*.

Journalist, historian and teacher, **James Murdoch** was the eminent Scottish scholar who was born in 1856 in Stonehaven, near Aberdeen.

From a humble background, he won a scholarship to study at Aberdeen University, later continuing his studies at the universities of Oxford, Paris and Göttingen.

Regarded by his contemporaries as a genius in foreign languages, including Sanskrit, he was aged 24 when he immigrated to Australia and taught for a time in Queensland.

He later worked for a period as a teacher of history in Tokyo, using his Japanese experiences to compile between 1903 and 1917 his magisterial three-volume *A History of Japan*; he died in 1921.

From the written word to architecture, **John Murdoch**, born in 1862 in Cassieford, Elgin was the Scottish architect who, after immigrating to Australia in 1884, went on to design many of the nation's iconic government buildings.

These included, before his death in 1945, the home of the Australian Parliament in Canberra.

Bearers of the Murdoch name have also been prominent in the worlds of science and invention, no less so than **William Murdoch**, also sometimes referred to as William Murdock, who is credited with the invention of gas lighting, the oscillating steam engine, the steam gun and many others.

Born the third of seven children in 1754 in Lugar, East Ayrshire, he was very much what is known as an ambitious Scottish 'lad o' pairts' – at the age of 24 walking the long distance from his native village to Birmingham to find employment with fellow Scots inventor James Watt.

Watt, along with his partner James Boulton, was engaged at the time in the manufacture of steam engines, and it was Murdoch who refined their technology to produce the oscillating steam engine.

His highly inventive mind also led him, between 1792 and 1794, while living in Redruth, Cornwall, to apply gas lighting in his home as replacement for what up until then had been light produced from candles.

In 1892, 53 years after his death, a bust of him was unveiled in the Wallace Monument in Stirling, while Redruth to this day holds an annual 'Murdoch Day.'

Equally inventive and someone who made a major contribution to the world of medicine, was the New Zealand pharmacist and veterinarian **Colin Murdoch**, born in 1929 in Christchurch.

Despite struggling with dyslexia as a young man, he went on to invent not only the disposable hypodermic syringe but also the childproof medicine container.

The winner of three gold medals at the 1976 World Inventions Fair in Brussels, he died in 2008.

No mention of the Murdochs could perhaps be complete without a reference to one of the most famous fictional bearers of the name.

This is Police Constable Joe Murdoch, better known as **P.C. Murdoch**, who, along with the comic characters Oor Wullie, Fat Boab, Wee Eck, Soapy Soutar and Ma and Pa, has delighted readers of the Scottish *Sunday Post* ever since 1936.